The Bad Day Book

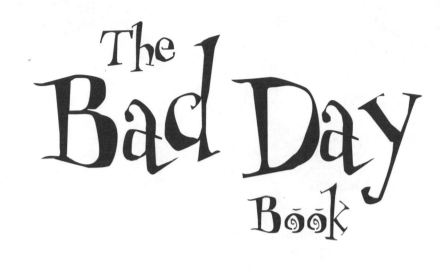

Guaranteed* to turn a rotten day into heavenly bliss

Ben Goode

Published by:
Apricot Press
Box 98
Nephi, Utah
84648

books@apricotpress.com
www.apricotpress.com

ISBN 1-885027-34-6

Illustrated & Designed by David Mecham
Printed in the United States of America

*The Apricot Press Guarantee

Actually, the guarantees you find in this book are probably not ours. My guess is they must have been put there by our dog, Odie. I wouldn't trust him as far as I can throw him since he lacks the ability to reason and he probably has no legal standing.

We at Apricot Press generally don't make guarantees because they just get us into trouble. About the only thing we promise is that if our stuff offends you, you can always give it to somebody you don't like.

Introduction

OK, so you're having a bad day, maybe a whole slew of them in rapid succession. You've tried whining, you've tried complaining and nobody cares. You've tried fantasizing, you've tried perspective, and while you may feel a little better for a while, you're still having a rotten day; you've tried overeating, anti-depressants, cable TV, violent video games, liberal politics, and other escapes and nothing seems to bring relief. After all this, you are just about to settle on abject, pitiful despair as the best solution when you stumble across this book and you think to yourself: "Finally, here is something I hadn't thought of: reading a book of booger humor."

But, sadly, having some really bad luck doesn't necessarily make a person stupid, irrational, or cause one to lose his or her ability to reason, and so you suspect that this book probably won't help much either. But since you can never be absolutely sure, you consider, "What if it WOULD make my days a little better and I dismissed it without even giving it a shot? What if there I am getting dumped on by the diarrhea plagued Emu of happiness when right there within my very grasp is the symbolic bottle of Kaopectate that will end all my misery and all I had to do was reach out and take it, but instead I put it back on the shelf and refused to symbolically suck the water out of the radiator when some nice person hands me a straw while I'm dying of thirst in the desert, all just because I have rational doubts? Come on! Get with the program! Have some faith in your fellow man! Get a little crazy! It's only $6.95!

- Ben Goode

Contents

Catching a skunk in your squirrel trap...

Ben Goode

How to be sure you're having a bad day

"Go ahead; have a bad day. You deserve it!" - Plato

Every day millions of people ask themselves, "Am I having a bad day?" While this is really a stupid question, it is, nonetheless, important because having a bona fide bad day can have some benefits. For example, it can give a person an excuse for being ornery, crabby, and rude to everyone around him. It's also important to know if you're having a bad day, because in the event you're NOT having a bad day, it can be proven mathematically that you must be having an OK day or maybe even a GOOD day, which could have important implications for you. It could mean your luck is changing, so now maybe instead of having things fall out of the sky onto your head and having your pets die, or instead of

1

winning the lottery but being unable to find the ticket, today you should consider mortgaging the house and betting the whole wad on whoever's playing the Yankees.

The fact is, if you're NOT having a bad day you may be having a "pretty good" day or even conceivably a "very good" day. This could be a rare opportunity to really annoy other people by getting a cheesy grin on your face and being obnoxiously cheery. Now, I'm not suggesting that you go hog wild or anything, especially if all you're having is a pretty good day. Frankly, you probably should go a little slow if you're making life-altering decisions, especially if you're doing it on the basis of what you're reading because this book is mostly a bunch of baloney. But, since we started out talking about whether or not you are in fact having a bad day, we better give you some clues. The following are some clues:

26 Sure Signs You Are Having A Bad Day*

(Those of you who enjoy reveling in misery may actually want to try some of these bad things on purpose to sort of start the ol' bad-day-ball rolling.)

1 - Today you catch a skunk in your squirrel trap.

2 - The Police officer who just pulled you over for a traffic ticket, suddenly runs back to his car and calls for backup.

3 - You wake up in the morning to find that your butt cheeks have mysteriously grown together.

4 - A new form of bacteria has been attacking your bank account.

5 - Seagulls score 37 direct hits on you during your walk from your car to the office where you're having your job interview.

6 - As you flush the toilet in the morning, half asleep; your thumb gets caught between the lever and the porcelain. It will require the entire fire department to free you.

7 - You wake up at 5:30 in the morning to the sensation of warm water splashing on your face. The source is your Great Dane, Sparky, who can't sleep because of his enlarged prostate, and he wants a snack.

8 - Just as you're leaving for work, your cat, Muffy, comes flying through the air hissing, lands on your face and scratches your ears into something that looks like angel hair pasta in meat sauce.

9 - You sit down for a quick breakfast before work and a football splashes onto your table since your kids are having a game in the kitchen.

10 - You sit down for breakfast and thousand of screaming Arabs surround your table making threatening gestures and screaming, "Down with you!" and "Death to you!"

11 - Hustling out to your car on the way to an important meeting, you grab your cell phone and lunch, and as an afterthought, you grab a chocolate candy bar, which you later figure out must have been a powerful laxative.

12 - The birds are chirping. You wake up and gaze longingly at your wife of 15 years. She gazes back just as the first rays of morning light burst through the window striking your beloved on her sculptured nose and turning her instantly into a bat.

13 - You watch on TV as your lottery numbers are called. TEN MILLION DOLLARS!!! You've finally won! Out of pure joy you run and leap out of the house, do a summersault off the porch, and instantly get flattened by a loaded garbage truck.

14 - While water skiing with friends, the Loch Ness monster hikes your shorts.

15 - You have been waiting for your car to be fixed. Just as the mechanic is letting it down on the jack, the instant the wheels hit the concrete, for some reason the jack explodes back up smashing your car flat against the garage roof.

*Note: Depending upon how you feel about your car, this could actually be an indication of a good day or maybe even a very good day.

16 - Sleeping out on the range, you are enjoying a spectacular meteor shower when one comes screaming to earth and makes an 80-foot-deep crater right where you used to be.

17 - You put your credit card into the ATM machine and get your money.

You glance up and notice you're surrounded by men in black.

18 - You put your card into the ATM machine and instead of cash a fake hand comes out and whacks you over the head with a rubber hammer.

19 - You put your card into the ATM and instead of cash, a flock of moths flies out.

20 - You put your card into the ATM and the $400.00 comes out shredded.

20.5 - You put your card into the ATM and instead of cash coming out you get a pie in the face.

21 - You put your card into the ATM and instead of cash a squirt gun comes out and hits you in the face.

22 - You put our card into the ATM, and instead of real cash, it gives you Monopoly money.

23 - You put your card into the ATM, a trap door opens, and half-a-ton of gerbil poop buries you.

24 - You take your seat on a full plane bound for Asia and sliding into the seat next to you is a man who looks a lot like a walrus and is that big, who, for his snack has a bag of garlic cloves.

25 - You wake up in the gutter to find a garbage truck parked on your lip.

26 - The giant they just transferred into your cell doesn't speak English or any other language you recognize.

Is This Bad Luck or Stupidity?

This is an important question. Bad luck is likely to change eventually; however, stupidity tends to persist. So, you might want to take the following test:

1. How long has your string of bad luck lasted?
   A. Just for today...so far.
   B. A week or two.
   C. As far as I know, through multiple reincarnations.

2. Do nice, well-meaning people try to help you?
   A. Occasionally.
   B. Frequently.
   C. Whenever you walk into a room everyone immediately drops whatever they're doing and grabs things on the shelves and walls?

3. Have you stopped eating with a fork because you keep jamming meatloaf into your eye?

4. Can you out drool your St Bernard?

5. Do your family members show their friends how the flashlight beam shines through both of your ears?

6. Sometime in your past, did you stop to think and then forget to start again?

Having taken this test, you are now in a position to analyze the results and hopefully determine whether your bad luck stems from genuine bad luck, or if you are having permanent bad luck because you are an idiot. Good luck.

Seven Indicators it could be a bad day if you're a COW

1. The milking machine is malfunctioning causing the amount of suction to quadruple.

2. The farmer came this morning to gently rub some balm on your now tender udders right after cutting up hot peppers.

3. You hear on the news that milk prices are plummeting and beef prices are soaring.

4. You are reminded today that the vet is coming to check your follicle.

5. Farmer Bob sprayed RoundUp on your pasture by mistake.

6. You have a recurring dream in which you see your face in the little dot pattern on a basketball.

7. Farmer Bob messed up again and fed the cows vegemite instead of corn silage.

Seven indications that a
DENTIST can expect a bad day:

1. Today's appointment schedule is filled entirely with people on strict "onions only" diets.

2. You just finished some masterful job on some fillings, you tell the patient to spit, and all his teeth come out into the little sink.

3. A group of your patients rise up in rebellion and start en mass drilling in your mouth as pay back.

4. Today it was announced that someone has invented and successfully

tested a new miracle pill to help people grow new teeth.

5. All your patients today are lawyers.

6. All your patients today are 3-year-old kids.

7. You have a bad crown in your mouth and have to go to the dentist for a root canal.

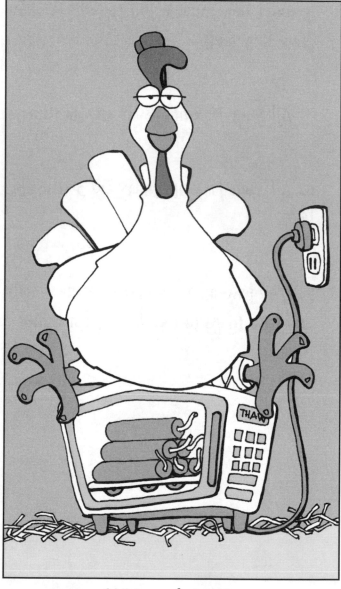

Child-proof dynamite

13 What are the causes of bad luck?

While it's true that there are many causes of bad luck, of course, the most common cause is being a meathead. Sadly, however, if we accuse everybody who buys this book of being a dork, it may have a negative effect on our sales, so, much like pop psych gurus we're going to pretty much avoid the hard stuff and try instead to give you what you want to hear. So for purposes of this book, whenever we talk about dorks and idiots, you can safely assume we're absolutely NOT talking about you. We are definitely talking about the other dorks and meatheads out there. Take for example the guy who can't get the child-proof packaging materials off from his dynamite so he can use it only as directed, so he shoves it into the microwave and puts the setting on "thaw" for

17

a few minutes thinking this will melt the glue and allow him to get into the package from the wrong side. What an idiot.

Some of you are way ahead of me here realizing the obvious fact that a match or lighter would do the same thing much faster while using less energy than a microwave but that's not the point. The point is you know this guy is going to blame the fact that his crew didn't get the road finished until after snow flew on his bad luck.

Now, the night shift guy who is sleeping in the back of the pick up truck filled with dynamite during all this could legitimately blame his hearing loss or death on his bad luck of being assigned to work with this other dim-wit, but we all know that the real reason is his own stupidity for taking a nap in the back of a truck at a construction site. As you all know, he is actually darned lucky that his buddies were too preoccupied with the child-proof packaging to notice that he was asleep, or he might have wound up with his shoe laces tied together or a frog in his lunch pail or even worse.

So, Where Does Bad Luck Come From?

(People are curious, so we provide this history.)

In the fall of 1776 a young Hessian farmer by the name of Rolf was weeding his cabbages and rutabagas on the Bavarian countryside dreaming of Wiener schnitzel, brown German beer and the lovely frau Jennifermeister.

Unbeknownst to him, the king, who we shall call king Rutherofrdstein III because his real name escapes us, was in deep financial doo doo. To the misfortune of thousands of young, military aged Bavarian guys, he had struck a deal with his cousin George III of England to receive a galleon-load of dough in exchange for sending a couple of boatloads of cannon fodder to help put down the rebellion in the British colonies.

Poor Rolf had the very bad luck of weeding alongside the road at the precise moment when the King's guard rode by looking for stout young men. They snatched him to go fight for God and country in the British colonies.

One might think this was unusually rotten luck and mumble something like, "Poor Rolf." This, however, actually turned into a spate of good luck on Rolf's part, since back in Bavaria, that very fall, the plague invaded the village, blight struck the rutabaga crop, his sweetie, Jennifermeister , it turns out, had been cheating on him with a plumber's assistant all along. Rolf, however, was able to keep all his happy, cherished memories of her untarnished because he was illiterate and couldn't read the letters from his Mom warning him about what a tart she was.

Fast forward to the winter of '78-'79. It was Christmas Eve and the Hessian infantry was hunkered down celebrating like a bunch of drunken college cheerleaders on spring break. Sadly, poor Rolf was outside freezing because he had guard duty. Since he was so large he needed a special sized uniform and since his uniform hadn't come, he had no choice but to wrap himself up in old tabloid newspapers and wrap his bleeding feet in rags and whatever else he could find to try and stay warm. To add insult to injury, it was raining and it was Christmas Eve. So, there he was freezing and dressed in rags at the precise time that Washington and his men crossed the Rubicon and launched the famous surprise attack heard round the world.

As Washington and his men sprung from their hiding places, Rolf jumped up in surprise, aimed his gun at the nearest Continental soldier and pulled the trigger. Since the Hessians couldn't afford training, his shot went wildly into the air killing a goose, which had been flying by. While this was very bad luck for the goose it turned out to be unusually good luck for Rolf because the Starving Continentals took one look at Rolf and assumed that because of his uniform he was one of them and that he was shooting the goose for Christmas dinner. And so Rolf ran around in total panic looking like a Continental soldier with an empty gun while all of his comrades were either killed or captured. Since they thought he was a Continental, and since he had shot the main course, when the shooting stopped, Rolf got to hang out and eat goose with the Americans, which, as it turns out was much more pleasant than being shot or captured.

So as you can see, you should never associate bad luck with bad luck because you can never really be sure it really is. It might actually be really good luck disguised as bad luck or it might be really bad luck disguised as moderately bad luck or something we haven't even thought of. In this case Rolf made some great buddies and ultimately decided to stay on and settle in New Jersey. Eventually, he married and changed his name to Rolf Springsteen and started a band with the squeezebox he made from his old foot rags. All this happened to him when he could have been hoeing rutabagas in Bavaria stressing over a philandering girl-friend and dying of the plague.

The other thing we can easily glean from this story is that the king caused much of Rolf's bad luck, and since the king is a politician, we can conclude that politicians, especially the President, cause much of the world's bad luck. Take for example my friend Cathy Murphy's wedding. Cathy and her groom chose for their wedding Memorial Day weekend because it was a government holiday and there was no school. After Cathy's parents spent over twenty thousand dollars for a blow out wedding on that particular Memorial Day, it rained cats and dogs. So you see, we need to hold those politicians responsible for everything bad that happens, especially the weather.

Seven Signs it may be a bad day if you're a CHICKEN:

1. If you wake up in the morning and find that you're hanging by your foot in China Town.

2. Hurrying to get dressed, you zip your feathers up in your pants.

3. The chicken below you, who has recently started smoking, wakes up in the middle of the night and catches your fine under feathers on fire.

4. You get all excited to lay another egg, but sadly, you discover that you just needed to go to the bathroom.

5. While you're pecking for bugs out in the yard, you notice out of the corner of your eye the KFC truck drive up and stop.

6. The farmer messed up and instead of putting you back in with all the hens for the night, he put you in the pen with one hundred and fifty roosters.

7. Having overslept in the morning at your hotel, you catch the first courtesy bus that comes along. Instead of going to the poultry show, you realize too late that you are on the bus headed for the weasel convention.

Eight Indicators That A TRUCK DRIVER Should Probably Expect a Bad Day:

1. You wake up to find that all the country radio stations have been replaced with rap and punk stations.

2. The price of diesel shoots up to over $2.00 per gallon.

3. You get a series of painful boils on top of your hemorrhoids.

4. The idiot brigade gets up early and is on the road from dawn till dusk and then they stay on the road all night.

5. You wake up in the morning in Hell and for your punishment you have to spend eternity following slow drivers.

6. You wake up in the morning in Hell and for your punishment you have to spend your life driving on roads that are always under construction.

7. You wake up in the morning in Hell and all the speed limits have been lowered and nobody told you...and the highway patrol force has been doubled.

8. Because you were talking to a friend and forgot to tip the waitress, she had the cook sneak out and let the air out of 17 of your 18 tires.

26 The fact that my waitress is
ignoring me is probably a good thing...

The Partial Cure: Self-Talk

One of the great secrets to getting along in life is having good, healthy self-talk. The way you talk to yourself can literally shape the words you mumble to yourself. In other words, if you're thinking unhappy thoughts, and you start muttering those disparaging comments about yourself to yourself, your subconscious mind may pick up on these and start giving your conscious mind those insults back again, and before you know it your Id steps in and picks a fight with your alter-ego, and then your right brain starts slugging it out with your left brain and visa versa, and without even trying you can become a psychological pile of frappe'ed moose dung, symbolically. So we think that your self-talk is very important. We recommend that whenever you are having a rotten day, instead of being honest with yourself and discussing these specifics with both cranial hemispheres, we suggest that you brighten your day by using happy self-talk like some of these phrases here.

Healing Bad-Day Self Talk:

1. "The fact that my waiter/waitress is ignoring me is probably a good thing on balance. It probably means she has forgotten about me and now he/she can give better service to other customers."

2. "If I hadn't overslept, I wouldn't be this rested – I am sharp!"

3. "The fact that the food is lousy here just means that I will probably eat less and therefore gain less weight."

4. "It seems the only phone calls I ever get are from telemarketers. At least while they're bothering me, they can't very well be bothering others who may be sick or infirm."

- Or -

"Actually, I've noticed that telemarketers have some similarities to my real friends."

5. "Being fired isn't all that bad. Until I starve to death, I can consider myself on vacation."

6. "Actually, it's probably a healthy thing for that guy to be flipping me off. It gives him an outlet for his anger other than shooting up the post office."

7. "I'm not really lost at all; This is a good thing because my being lost now will help me learn to find my way around and possibly even prevent my being lost here in the future."

8. If you totaled your car: "Until I get another one, me and everyone on the road will be just a little bit safer."

- Or -

"This is great! My fuel and maintenance expenses will go way down for a while."

- Or -

"It's probably a good thing that, for a while at least, I'm not buying gas from people who are bent on America's destruction."

9. When you're being tax-audited: "It's a real honor to be selected out of millions of people—kind of like the lottery."

- Or -

"I'll bet he's on a quest to find the perfect books; I'll bet my books will get him closer to realizing that goal than he's ever been before."

10. On the days when you discover your favorite pet has been transformed into a little furry road Frisbee: "Finally, Sparky will no longer suffer from the humiliation of being called 'a dog.'"

- Or -

"He looks so peaceful. I'll bet he was

having a great time chasing that cat pizza over there and this way the fun can go on in heaven.

11. On bad hair days: "Now I can be absolutely sure that people will like me for who I am and not just for my hair."

- Or -

"At least I have nice hair on my arms."

12. When I get pulled over and get a ticket: "Actually, I'm grateful they caught me now-this could have led to some really big crimes like parking in handi-capped zones or even swerving to hit a cat."

- Or -

"This is really a great thing I'm doing, paying for this ticket will contribute to the economy and make it possible for the legislators to reduce the tax burden on other citizens."

13. If you've lost all your friends: "The voices in my head are more fun than real people anyway."

- Or -

"Now I can go after her boyfriend (or his girlfriend) with abandon and a clear conscience."

14. When you're stranded at the checkout counter with $300.00 of stuff and your credit card is rejected: "I'll bet that when compared to most of the

The Bad Day Book

other crooks and deadbeats who get their
credit cards rejected I'm a pretty solid
guy. I wonder what my ranking would
be."

15. "If people like me didn't speed,
these nice police persons would have
nothing to do."

....

Trite clichés about your rotten
luck that probably won't change
anything, but may make you feel
better

"Enjoy your bad days and they will
enjoy you."

- Eugene Voltaire

"There is no such thing as a bad day, only 24 hour blocks of time in which a whole bunch of rotten things happen."

- Jack Thoreau

"Learn to appreciate your bad days for what they are, segments of time when things are really lousy."

- Earl Whippoorwill

"You think you're having a bad day, try being burned at the stake."

- Joan of Arc

"A lousy day is like a lousy week - only shorter."

- Bogi Yerra

Seven signs of possible pending bad luck if you're a DOG:

1. You are the picture of health, wet nose, shiny coat and everything; nothing is wrong with you—and yet your owner is taking you to the vet.

2. As luck would have it, this time the person's crotch you're sniffing hasn't showered for a couple of weeks...and just passed gas.

3. Your owners are gone for the day and while they were considerate enough to leave the toilet seat up, they forgot to flush.

4. The car you are chasing makes a sharp turn and narrowly avoids a collision with a garbage truck. You don't.

5. The gorgeous Pomeranian who just moved in up the street, upon closer inspection, turns out to be a male Pigmy goat.

6. You find the remains of the beautiful Pomeranian who just moved in up the street with diesel truck tires from end to end and it's probably now only useful as a decoration on your doghouse wall or to gnaw on to clean your teeth.

7. While marking your territory last night, you marked an electric fence.

Cleo Caesar

13 Five wretched examples of bad luck in history

Bad luck has been around a long time, longer than I can remember. We have included this chapter just to give you a few examples:

Example #1

Cleo Caesar, last of the Caesars' daughter, planned her wedding to be the social event of the millennium in Rome. Cleo and her fiancé' Earlicus Stoutamus had just finished their first round of the banquet and were headed for the vomitorium when, as luck would have it, a hoard of Vandals rode up with a million horsemen. The invaders immediately began pillaging right in the middle of the second course and to make matters worse, they were eating all the food, even the stuff that was supposed to be saved for later.

Because it's tough to pillage on an uncomfortably full stomach, the German tribal leaders asked the hostess for bags to put the leftovers in. (This is where the term, "sacking Rome" came from.) To make matters even worse, before the invaders could finish off all the food, it started to rain. Since all the important government officials were at the wedding and therefore busy being pillaged, there was no one to answer the phone when someone called to let them know that the rain and the Vandals had caused the sewers of Rome to back up. Since the sewers were backed up there was nowhere for the guests or the Vandals to use the bathroom, which made the invaders even more surly. Before we knew it, the entire Roman Empire had collapsed into anarchy.

Example #2

Adam and Eve had just finished plans for a summer home but before they got to enjoy it, they got kicked out of the garden.

Example #3

Long ago, in Ancient Egypt the first Pharaoh was building this huge palace and just before the cement could dry it rained for the first time in ten years causing this enormous cement lump walls to collapse. This gargantuan cement mass that was now partly dry was too heavy to move, and who wants this huge lump of rock in the front yard? Certainly not the Pharaoh! The dejected potentate couldn't think of anything else to do, so he ordered the royal architect to have the stone masons take it apart chipping away one chisel at a time. As a joke, out of boredom, just goofing around, the stonemasons chiseled the lump into a huge cat and put the pharaoh's bust on top as a joke on the architect. The architect's body has never been found.

Example #4

In Germany during the election of 1932, Adolph Schnitzler was running for Chancellor on the Democratic ticket. Unluckily, his name was misspelled on the ballot to read "Adolph Hitzler." Adolph won the election, but when he brought in his paperwork to claim his job, the name on his driver's license didn't match the name on the ballot, so the government campaign officials rudely sent him home dejected. Meanwhile, Adolph Hitler, who had only run as a joke, and had only received 3 votes, was sitting at home editing his copy of Mein Kampf, which had been a commercial failure, into a self help book on gardening. It was pathetic try and get something going in his life.

While watching the election returns on the TV news it suddenly occurred to him that the chancellor elect's name was very similar to his own and so got this bright idea. He thought it would be a great gag to go and claim the chancellorship of Germany. As luck would have it, the election officials had just been chewed out by one of their wives for being so rude to nice Herr Schnitzler, and so they were feeling a little guilty. Not wanting to get chewed out again, they were determined to be a little more courteous this time and so when Adolph Hitler came in, since his name was pretty close, they gave him the job without even showing I.D. This turned out to be some bad luck for pretty much the rest of the world.

Example #5

The Greeks ordered a huge decorator catapult to help break the siege with the Trojans. The clerk, Obeisethenese, who actually placed the order accidentally misspelled the shipping address to read 110 Achilles Avenue, which, everyone knows is in New Jersey, so naturally, that's where the manufacturer shipped the catapult. When the Trojan horse showed up at the siege six months later, the Defenders of the city just figured the catapult manufacturer was slow and besides they thought the horse motif was pretty trendy for a catapult so they let it in. So while their catapult ended up a classical amusement park ride in Yonkers, the Trojans took credit for a huge military victory after what should have just been a weak gag.

I could go on and on, but what would be the point? We all know that bad luck has a long history, so let's move on.

Four Ominous signs of a bad day if you're a MARSHMALLOW:

1. You find yourself packed in the station wagon along-side the roaster sticks and wieners.

2. You are accidentally dropped, and suddenly find yourself lying near an ant bed.

3. You wind up in the tread of someone's shoe.

4. You find yourself inside someone's stomach all mixed up with a chimichanga, salsa, and refried beans.

How to tell if a SPIDER is going to have a bad day:

1. He spins his web in front of a pitching machine and then takes a nap.

2. He happens to be the unlucky spider that, while minding his own business, stumbles across the path of a 4-year-old boy who has been spending the morning pulling the legs off every bug he could catch.

3. The wind blows him and his web into a chicken coop.

4. He crawls inside someone's boot to take a nap just before they wake up.

5. The spout that this itsy, bitsy spider crawls up turns out to be the barrel of a shotgun.

6. A farmer drops off 50 chickens into the yard where he has just spun his web.

7. The farm family who owns your friend, the pig, has become convinced that the messages you've been writing in your web indicate that the pig is possessed, so they sneak up when he's not looking and blast him with a rocket launcher.

Clues that an AIRLINE PILOT could be headed for a bad day:

1. Your right engine falls off right after your left engine bursts into flames. The only working engine you know of is the one in your electric razor, and you're pretty sure it's in the baggage compartment.

2. Upon switching over to your reserve fuel tank, you discover that the ground service crew filled it with champagne as a practical joke.

3. You glance in your rear-view mirrors just in time to see your co pilot, who just excused himself to go to the potty,

disappear into a cloud, apparently having just been sucked through the privy into space.

4. Upon take-off, you get off just in time to see a spectacular view of the sky in front of you being blackened by an enormous flock of chickens.

5. You just woke up from a good daydream to discover that you have inadvertently drifted directly over the White House. Ten F-16's and a heat-seeking missile are now aggressively pursuing you.

Being lost at sea on a cruise ship...

13 Illegitimate reasons for having a bad day

Since there are plenty of legitimate reasons to have a bad day, we here at Apricot Press think it's pretty schenky of some of you to have rotten days for weak reasons.

The following are some illegitimate reasons for having a bad day. If you are having a bad day and you're blaming one of the following causes, whatever you do don't whine to the rest of us.

The following would be some of those illegitimate reasons for having a bad day:

-The local Rolls Royce dealer is moving this week. He just happens to have a

few cars unsold from his big parking-lot
sale with the giant inflated gorilla and he
doesn't want to move them. The dealer
called and wants to know if you want to
come and pick one up for free, but you
will have to maintain it.

-While on a cruise, the captain of the
ship gets lost, and it looks like it will
take a few more weeks for him to find
his way home.

-Brittney Spears, Julia Roberts, Nicole
Kiddman all specifically ask for you to
be the stand-in for all of the love
scenes in their new movies. (Actually,
now that I think of it, if you're married
or a girl, this could be a pretty good

reason to have a bad day. So, go ahead if you want to on this one, but at least do it with high self-esteem.)

-This year you dropped two positions in the Forbes 500-Richest-People-In-The-World list.

-A new drug has just been discovered to make you feel and look like you're 20 regardless of your age...and as a side effect, you may live forever.

-The Chippendale calendar guys just volunteered to give your house a thorough cleaning twice a week just to be nice.

The snooze button hallucination...

Irrational thoughts and their effect on bad days

Sadly, one of the main reasons for bad days is totally unrealistic expectations. No matter how good your day is turning out, if you were expecting better things, you will be disappointed and consider it a bad day. As an eminent bad-day expert professional and author, I, therefore, suggest that you get your thinking in line. The lower your expectations, the better your days, it would seem to me. I have noticed over the years that many people have stupid expectations that just set them up for failure, disappointment and bad days. I would like to help you with those expectations and so I give you Stephen Glenn, quoting Albert Einstein, Yogi Berra or somebody who once said, "The definition of a crazy person is one who continues to do the same things, yet expects different results." Despite pretty obvious facts, many people wait for things to happen that aren't going to. To help you lower your expectations we give you:

Common Hallucinations

(Bogus things crazy people believe)

1. I'm going to hit snooze and sleep for another five minutes. This will make me feel better.

2. My coworkers are genuinely interested in my complaints and problems.

3. My kids will never act like that.

4. If we try to act like the Europeans, they will think we're cool.

5. My ship is out there somewhere.

6. If we common people try to act like famous people, they will think we're cool.

7. If I knock myself out to make other people think I'm cool, they will think I'm cool.

8. Other people like to be around my kids.

9. If we give the government this tax increase then they will be happy and content and will not ask for more.

If you are the DICTATOR of a third-world country, these are seven indicators that it might be a bad day for you:

1. The doctor who is about to perform your emergency heart bypass surgery turns out to be the father of one of the political prisoners being tortured in the other room.

2. One of your concubines, who recently escaped, is being interviewed by Katie Couric.

3. The U.S. Marines have discovered your bunker and you don't know it.

4. Your closest friend figures out a way to poison you without being caught.

5. You and a thousand concubines are chillin' in the huge palatial bunker miles beneath the surface of the earth when the sewer clogs up.

6. Your dopey, lazy slug of a son figures out all the cool things he gets to do once you're dead and he gets to run the show without your interference.

7. The market for illegal drugs drops to the point that your country has to figure out a way to make it's living supplying the only other thing your country produces for export: rubber chickens.

Nine major indicators it's going to be a bad day if you are a RABBIT:

1. As you limp into the truck stop on your crutches, you spot some good luck charms that look familiar.

2. You read in the newspaper that the hawk and eagle populations are soaring.

3. A family of snakes moves into the burrow next door.

4. Last year while you were inebriated and using poor judgment, you agreed to have Easter coincide with the first day of hunting season.

5. Rabbit fur shoes and underwear becomes the rage among teenagers worldwide.

6. Word gets out that you taste like chicken.

7. All 15 of your children get together and demand that the only things they want to eat are raisins.

8. Fast food joints start adding rabbit to their menus as a healthy alternative to chicken.

9. The woman who buys you from the pet store is a kindergarten teacher.

How to get the most from your rotten luck

We know how it really stinks to be walking somewhere, minding your own business when out of nowhere a piano falls on top of you and you didn't even happen to be stepping over a manhole. That's why when you have truly rotten luck you need to do all you can to use your luck to your advantage. One of the great useful uses for bad luck is to plague irritating people, who would otherwise have pretty good luck if you weren't standing nearby. It stands to reason that if you have really rotten luck and hang around annoying people, chances are some of your lousy luck will slop over onto them. This can be good.

For example, I have a friend, Farley, who is plagued by rotten luck. Most of us who know him are aware of this and keep our distance most of the time. One day Farley was walking by the mink sheds eating a can of Vienna Sausages just at the precise moment when a group of adolescent animal rights terrorists were opening the pens to let them out. As Farley's luck would have it, at that instant an earthquake of 6.5 magnitude struck. Thanks in part to Farley's rotten luck, the large crack that ran through the mink farm swallowed up the terrorists. Since Farley has become used to such luck, he was prepared. He grabbed a board and stretched it across the crevasse and as soon as the shaking stopped, crawled out and was on his way. The terrorists, on the other hand, wound up digging their way out and eventually surfaced in the cave of some REAL terrorists in Afghanistan. We have no record of what happened next, but it is clear that their lives were significantly impacted by Farley's bad luck, probably for the benefit of society at large.

Naturally, it was too late to stop the mink from getting out and of course, a couple thousand of them attacked Farley to get the Vienna Sausages, and then of course, while he was wallowing there on the ground, the skunks came along with some weasels and a badger and joined in and before he could do anything about it they had pretty much ruined his new bowling shoes. But it's probably too much to expect people to use ALL of their bad luck to benefit others, some is bound to still attack the innocent, especially if this person is REALLY unlucky.

How to Apply Your Bad Luck

Fortunately, if you are one who suffers from freakishly bad luck, and who has had this bad luck for an extremely long time, you owe it to your country to do everything you can to contribute in every way possible to improve your community. For example, you might consider helping to thin out the lawyer population. This would be a real service. If you were to grab a pair of water wings and go sit in court somewhere in Idaho. While you're watching the A.C.L.U. argue for coyote's rights to eat rancher's sheep or for some Junior High kids' right to produce child pornography using the school's computers, if you stay long enough, with your luck, something's horrible is bound to happen to everyone in the courtroom including the evil lawyers. For example, if a tsunami hits, you can ride it out farther East and then maybe stay on in Colorado and hang around the University's law School for a while or even go grab a hot dog from the vender in front of the building that houses the state bar. Better yet, go on in and see if you can find an ambulance chaser to try to get you a settlement for one of the disasters you've been a part of during the past week. While they're meeting with you trying to determine how much money they can make, all kinds of cool things could happen, who knows? Whatever you do, avoid bookstores and printing establishments unless they produce competing booger humor. If you run across any of those, take them a sandwich and hang around for a while. In this way, you might do a great amount of good for your country.

Seven Indicators that you are Probably going to have a bad day if you are a DUCK

1. Today you finally realized you will not be turning into a swan.

2. You just found out that you have been the only one who didn't know that your role model and hero is a Disney Character. For all these years you've been running around without pants thinking it was cool.

3. You just discovered today that you have a very limited future because you are poultry with no formal education.

4. The explosions and flack coming from down below tells you that what you thought were buddies on the pond down below are probably wooden decoys.

5. You woke up this morning plucked and hanging in an Asian market.

6. The farmer who owns you just changed your diet to grain.

7. The alligator swimming down below is a practical joker. He has wedged your foot between a couple of rocks so he can come back periodically to tickle you...and take a bite out of your drumstick.

Sprint home, lock the doors, and
cower in bed...

13 More things you can do whenever you're having a bad day

"So, I'm having a rotten day. Just what can I do about it?" You ask. If you are asking this, you obviously didn't read the last chapter, but since we have some other ideas, that's OK. You can read this one anyway. I've thought quite a bit about this question myself lately since I'm writing a book on the subject, and I've decided that you do have some options. Unfortunately, none of them are any good and will probably just make things a whole lot worse, but, at least if I tell you about them, you can't whine about not having any options.

For example, as soon as you are certain you are having a bad day, you could sprint back home, lock all the doors, and cower in your bed. (See, I told you these were not great options.) If you are really having a bad day, your dog will jump up on you in your bed, and while licking your face have diarrhea all over your sheets; then, while you're gagging as you clean up the mess, the roof will start leaking, the toilet will clog, and the only mail you will get will be a bacteria laced letter from a terrorist or an unusually large credit card bill. Then, your electricity will short out and your house will burn down so you can clearly see that this is not the best option.

Another thing you can do when having a bad day is dress up in your Woody Woodpecker costume and run around screaming, "The sky is falling!" While this won't help anything, it will get you committed to one of your finer mental institutions for a few weeks at least, release a little tension, and help you feel exhilarated until they put the straight jacket on you. On the other hand, it might get you elected to Congress or The Senate or hired to work on Ralph Nader's staff or something; it will certainly get most of the senior citizen vote and if you can't get yourself elected with all those votes, you better move to Florida.

If you want to get extra creative, you can write your congressman or the president and whine to them. As long as you contributed a few million to their campaign and are from a big state that matters on Election Day, they will at least have an insignificant staff person listen to you for a while and nod her head in sympathy.

Still some other ideas, which won't fix anything but which might not make things too much worse would be to squirt grapes or watermelon seeds at your coworkers or to lie down in the road, and complain until everybody goes away. While these are pretty lame suggestions, you can be firm in the knowledge that we have now completed another chapter and are well on our way to finishing this entire book. Thanks.

Evidence today may be a bad day if you're a CAT.

1. You wake up in the morning, yawn and stretch, and then suddenly realize you're inside a gunnysack at the bottom of the canal.

2. The little girl who owns you has a party; they decide to play dolls and you're it.

3. While lost in a daydream, you suddenly realize that your 9th spirit is hovering above a furry road pizza.

4. The people who owned you just accidentally hooked your flea collar to

the bumper of a pizza delivery truck.

5. As you slowly drain your milk saucer, savoring every lick, a stinkbug thorax gradually emerges.

6. While you were napping, mad scientists have attached electrodes to your underbelly.

7. While sleeping in the sun of the big window, your fluffy fur explodes into flames from spontaneous combustion. In fifteen seconds you look like a smoldering naked wiener dog.

Geeks are taking over...

13 How to turn your rotten luck around

*(After those last two chapters, it is hard for me to
understand why anyone would want to change his or
her luck, but just in case someone wants this information,
like the professional journalist I am, I will deliver.)*

As I travel around in my pickup truck I meet many
people who are plagued with awful luck. Over and over
again they tell me things like, "Your fly is open," "You
have something gross in your teeth," and "Why don't
you do something with your life that would actually
benefit mankind or something?" or "In the big scheme
of things, what exactly is the value of booger humor?"

Even though most of these people are idiots and are
probably in no position to make any value judgment

about someone else's career because their life is a train wreck, my theory is that what they are really asking is, "How can I turn this bad luck around and make it good luck?" In other words, "Do you know the winning numbers to the lottery or any other way to beat the system so I can avoid having to change the character flaws in my life so I actually deserve better luck?"

So, in answer to these important questions my response would be something like, " Our over-all luck in this country has become so horrible that is now to the point that geeks are taking over. You know this is true. A case in point: just a few short years ago you hardly ever even saw a geek. They all pretty much stayed out of sight fiddling with gadgets, playing with their Rubik's Cubes or playing chess. Today they are everywhere. You can't avoid them because thanks to the direction technology has taken; no business can be without them. Frustrated business people like me who have high blood pressure from trying to fix their own computer problems have literally dragged every geek they know out of the closet by their pocket protectors squeaking and whining because we can't function without them. Everybody nowadays must have a geek, dweeb, nerd, or some similar technician to fix our computers because our business has become completely and totally dependent upon them. We can no longer do the slightest bit of business without our computers. I think they planned it this way.

Fortunately, the geeks I know have some cool, redeeming qualities; like that they are gullible and fun to tease. For example, the other day we told our resident geek that the only path through the dungeon and around the swamp where you had even the slightest chance of rescuing the princess was available if you jumped over the pylons and through portal Q and that was only available to programmers who could merge their D.O.S. software with a Mac while twirling their machine at gyro repetitions. He subsequently spent the next fortnight trying to prove me wrong.

So whenever I get thinking that life is rotten I just pull a prank on a geek and it makes me feel better. As far as finding ways to turn a person's rotten luck around, nobody around here has a clue about that, so we just bail out psychologically and emotionally by playing practical jokes. Cheers!

If you're a WEASEL you should probably expect a bad day if:

1. You suddenly develop a conscience.

2. Your pollsters tell you that instead of viewing "getting along" as a good thing, your constituency expects you to have some principles if you're to be re-elected.

3. Using a complex formula your constituents cut your salary to the average of what they make.

4. You have a rare disease and every time you lie the boil on your butt grows bigger and erupts.

5. Your pollsters tell you that your constituents are finally getting wise to the fact that you're just using their own money to buy their votes.

6. The voters pass a referendum requiring you to obey the same laws they have to.

7. They pass term limits.

8. You develop a psychological condition where you are unable to lie.

Just one curse would have been enough for most of us

Ben Goode

 **Is there a connection between bad luck and stupidity**

If you are wondering this right now you should probably be aware that those people who you thought were your friends probably only want you around when they need someone to lend them money, or someone upon which to play their favorite practical joke (See chapter 13).

While it is true that stupid people generally have a disproportionately high percentage of bad days, there is one group who has even worse luck. This group is made up of those people who have managed to really make God angry with them. They tend to pretty much have all bad days. Take for example Pharaoh of Egypt who kept promising to let the good guys go and then re-negged a dozen times so that every day he woke up to a new curse. What an idiot! Just one curse would have been enough for most of us, but not Pharaoh. He had to try them all. Many of you would ask, "What kind of Gomer would do that?" And so we see that in this case stupidity is still partly the culprit, though I'm sure that if we think for a while we can come up with a famous example of someone who made God angry and wasn't stupid, but let's move on and look at some other examples.

Some examples of people who have bad luck because they must have made God angry:

- The people living in the walled city of Jericho
- Lot's Wife
- The residents of Sodom and Gomorrah
- The residents of Pompeii
- Chicago Cubs Fans
- Christians during ancient Rome

- Republicans During the Clinton Years
- The L.A. Clippers
- Jack-In-The Box Restaurants
- Hollywood marriages
- Friends of the President
- People named Dick
- People who bought pet rocks

While we're looking at stupidity we better take a look at another major cause of bad luck and bad days which can be even more insidious: INSANITY. Many of you are undoubtedly familiar with many of the common mental illnesses. (The fact that you're reading this book could be an indication that you are REALLY familiar with them.) These include: Neurosis, Depression, Adolescent Psychosis, Delusions of Grandeur, Bipolar Ice Caps, Telemarketing, Sado-Masochism, Hip Hop, Pyromania, Rhythm and Blues and Road Rage, just to name a few. And of course, science is coming up with new ones everyday, which are not yet exempted from your insurance coverage.

If you happen to suffer from one of these illnesses or even if you are really weird and suffer from one not yet discovered, and you suffer from bad luck or are having a bad day, please read chapter 13 for more ideas about what you can do.

The following indicate you may be headed for a bad day if you're a WAITRESS:

1. When you arrive at work, the chef informs you that he is out of everything on the menu except for mushrooms and Spam.

2. Tonight is Prom night at the local high school.

3. The blisters on your feet that popped yesterday grew blisters.

4. It's July and the air conditioner in the restaurant will only blow hot air.

5. Today there is a meeting of the lame joke convention at your restaurant.

6. Unbeknownst to you, all the soft drinks in the joint are loaded with triple caffeine.

7. All the regulars arrive today earlier than usual in the morning and promptly inform you they have nothing to do all day.

8. The cook's wife left him for another man and so he's lashing out by sabotaging everyone's meals with strange surprises.

Fishing with dynamite therapy

Ben Goode

13 The effects of fishing on foreign policy

Experts[1] believe that we would have many fewer problems in the world if world leaders all knew how to fish. This is especially true in the Middle East where they seem to have all the biggest problems. Experts[2] believe this is because they don't have hardly any water to fish in, and so they get so stressed out they blow themselves up.

This is why many government leaders[3] have begun denying seats in the United Nations to countries whose

---

[1] Most of these people are experts on things like plumbing and pumping gas, but they are, nonetheless experts.

[2] These too.

[3] These would be leaders of Junior High School governments for the most part.

leaders don't fish. We think this is a good idea. In fact, we heartily endorse this policy and would even like to expand on it a little bit. For example, we think it would be a good idea to deny drivers licenses to people who don't fish. This is completely logical if you think about it, because it is impossible to have a bad day while you're fishing, and since the roads are so full of idiots it's just about impossible to have a GOOD day driving, especially in traffic where the ratio of considerate, intelligent drivers to idiots is 86 to one. Since the crazies in The Middle East are generally wasting their dynamite by blowing up nice people who travel on busses instead of blowing up idiotic drivers who probably deserve it, we would like to suggest that they could relieve their tension in a less destructive way AND get rid of all their unwanted dynamite, which seems to be everywhere in the Middle East, if they were to try using dynamite to fish. I personally did this a couple of times back in the early 70's when fishing with dynamite was still legal in most states and me and my high school buddies had great fishing success. In fact, we could get upwards of 20 or 30 carp to surface with just one stick of dynamite properly placed. I would also like to point out that fishing with dynamite is relaxing and therapeutic. It seems to me that this idea of fishing diplomacy could lead to fewer conflicts in the world thus making diplomacy much easier. Imagine diplomats from different countries handling their countries' business while fishing.

I can see it all now. The American Ambassador would cast his fly gently into the sweet spot near the far bank as he pitched his proposal to his counterpart from some Arab country who, while taking a moment to consider the proposal would completely relax as he reached into his backpack and grabbed a stick of dynamite, lit it and lobbed it into the hole by the willows near the far bank. Using this procedure, I think there would be little grounds for disagreement or strife because they would be having such a great time gathering up the fish, which would be floating by the bushel baskets full on the surface of the water, and in addition, fewer people would have bad days.

*NOTE: The following has nothing to do with having a bad day. OK, maybe a little, but it has been put in here anyway because we needed a little extra material to fill it up.

Some wonderful happy statements that, sadly, you will not live long enough to hear.

1. "We've pretty much fixed all the roads in the state so there won't need to be any construction this summer."

The State Department of Transportation

2. "You tax payers have sacrificed enough over the years. It wouldn't be right for us to ask for any more of your hard earned money."

The Government

3. "Since I couldn't make you better, I am giving you a refund of all your money and insurance premiums."

The Doctor/Hospital

4. "This social program hasn't made the problem much better, certainly not enough to justify the enormous cost, in fact, it might even have made it worse, so we're going to end it."

Your Legislators

5. "Yeah, I guess that outfit does make you look fat."

Your Husband.

6. "Mosquitoes and intestinal parasites are animals and they have rights just like the cute ones."

PETA

7. "My opponent has some really good ideas, and if I'm elected I plan to implement many of them."

Political Candidate

8. "There are lots of problems with the schools that aren't about money. We won't ask for any tax increases until we

Prove we can do a better job using the
money we've already generously been
given."

The NEA and your school board

9. "My opponent is a decent, honorable,
intelligent person."

Political candidate

10. "I would just be wasting your money if
I charged you for anything; your teeth are
in great shape."

Your dentist

11. "Yes, I know our music is really, really
bad technically and any fool can see that it
has a terrible destructive effect on

adolescent children, but we're going to keep doing it so we can get richer."

Rap, Hip Hop and Rock Musicians and executives

12. "Thanks, and by the way we're doing just fine now and won't need any more of your foreign aid."

Foreign Countries

13. "Thanks to your introspection, awareness and sacrifices, we have been able to make huge progress. We have finally reached the point where our group no longer needs any special treatment."

Minority and Women's' Rights activist

'The Truth About Life' Humor Books

Order Online! www.apricotpress.com

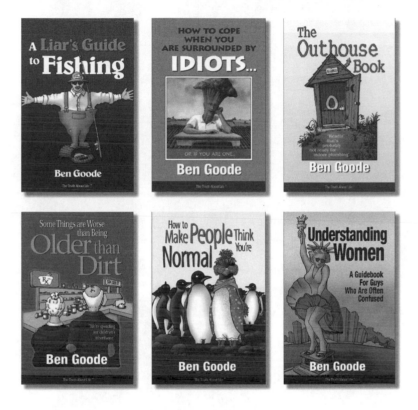

Apricot Press Order Form

Book Title	Quantity	x	Cost / Book	=	Total
_____	_____		_____		_____
_____	_____		_____		_____
_____	_____		_____		_____
_____	_____		_____		_____
_____	_____		_____		_____
_____	_____		_____		_____
_____	_____		_____		_____
_____	_____		_____		_____

All humor books are $6.95 US.

Do not send Cash. Mail check or money order to:
**Apricot Press   P.O. Box 98
Nephi, Utah   84648**
Telephone 435-623-1929
Allow 3 weeks for delivery.

**Quantity discounts available.
Call us for more information.**
9 a.m. - 5 p.m. MST

Sub Total =

Shipping = $2.00

Tax 8.5% =

Total Amount
Enclosed =

Shipping Address

Name:

Street:

City: State:

Zip Code:

Telephone:

Email: